Voices From The Clouds
A collection of 125 poems

by

Adegoke Unimke Oyegade

An AuthorsOnLine Book

Published by Authors OnLine Ltd 2003

Copyright © Authors OnLine Ltd

Text Copyright © Adegoke Unimke Oyegade 2003

The moral right of the author has been asserted

All rights reserved. No part of this publication may be reproduced, stored in a retrieval system, or transmitted in any form or by any means, electronic, mechanical, photocopy, recording or otherwise, without prior written permission of the copyright owner. Nor can it be circulated in any form of binding or cover other than that in which it is published and without similar condition including this condition being imposed on a subsequent purchaser.

ISBN 0-7552-0073-X

Authors OnLine Ltd
15-17 Maidenhead Street
Hertford SG14 1DW
England

This book is also available in e-book format from
www.authorsonline.co.uk

About the author

Adegoke Unimke Oyegade is a medical doctor who graduated from the University of Ilorin Medical School, Nigeria, in 1987. He is married to Doris and they have a son, Daniel. They now live in Manchester, England.

He developed a passion for creative writing while in the secondary school. Voices From The Clouds is his first collection of poems. Currently he is working on another collection of poems, a novel and a collection of personal quotations.

He is no doubt aspiring to emerge as an outstanding voice in the literary world.

Contents

A Tribute to R.S. Thomas	1	Sentiment	48
Poverty	2	Habits	49
Crime Has No Colour	3	The Colour Of Justice	50
Anger	4	The Crafty Politician	51
The Battle of Life	5	A Day in Winter	52
The Human Mind	6	Have A Dream	53
Can't Have Your Way Always	7	I know I know	54
Dreamland	8	Disappointments	55
Hatred	9	The Contrasting Veils	56
Fear	10	Midnight Hour of Life	57
The Human Face	11	Late Wishes	58
Technology	12	Empty	59
A Fool As A Prince	13	The Songs of Birds	60
Tears From The Eyes	14	Food	61
Thinking Astray About Thinking	15	Noise	62
Body, Soul and Spirit	16	Voice of Bias	63
Racism A Canker	17	Lazy Brats	64
The Strange Intruder	19	Failures	65
Love Turned Sour	20	Imagination	66
Death The Caller	21	Were He Not Born	67
Memories	22	Man and the Environment	68
The Violent	23	Not Meant To Be	69
Hard Drugs	24	Blossoming At Night	70
Twisted Personalities	25	God Near or Far	71
Vengeance	26	Reflection	72
Conscience	27	The Crafty Man	73
Believe In Yourself	28	He Had Not A Home	74
Truth Is Unsoothing	29	Change	75
Indulgence	30	Veil Upon The Heart	76
Suffering	31	Governed By What?	77
Risk	32	Psychological Nourishment	78
Solitude	33	The Hospital	79
The Pressures of Life	34	Dying Before Their Time	80
Discouragement	35	Man A Complex	81
The Eyes A Window	36	She Knew Not She Had It	82
Disease	37	The Wind	83
Boomerang	38	The Quaking Earth	84
No Perfection	39	In A Vast Landscape	85
Complex Variables	40	Flowers	86
Believe in the Future	41	The Aeroplane	87
Arrogance	42	In My Distress	88
The Arm of the Law	43	The Age Of Wisdom	89
My Love Insect	44	The Battle Never To Be Won	90
A Ray Of Hope	45	The Prolific Writer	91
The Limiting Factor	46	Moonlight	92
The Sun	47	Seeking Rest	93

The Young Man's Confusion	94	Silenced	110
The Beggar	95	The Animal I Like	111
The Contradiction Of Joy	96	Guilt	112
The Sides Of The Truth	97	Vain Search	113
The Doctor I Know	98	Malice	114
Inequality	99	Living In the Past	115
The Stillborn	100	Obsession	116
Rain	101	Tinted	117
The Silent Evening Cloud	102	Victims Of Crime	118
Good Music	103	Injustice	119
Entangled	104	Emotion	120
Not Alone In The Boat	105	The Voice of Prejudice	121
Seeking Answers	106	The Colourless Man	122
Man	107	In A Moment Of Madness	123
Psychological Warfare	107	The Poet	124
A Child - Joy In The Home	108	Man and Woman	125
Water	109		

Preface

This collection of 125 poems covers a wide range of themes, spanning from the simple to the complex, all of which have a spice of contemporary reality.

I challenge my readership to come with me on a voyage of poetic excitement and reasoning; one not without a price. But it will be worth the effort, if we come out better informed and transformed.

It is hoped that this collection will help fan the dying or burning embers of your love of poetry into blazing flames. I believe that the lucidity of expression which has been brought to play in the poems will help to achieve this.

Voices From The Clouds
A collection of 125 poems

A Tribute to R.S. Thomas

A poetry legend he was
A man of letters
Volumes there are to his credit
Exuding quiet character and inner strength
A man of poetic diversity
A man of conviction.

A great poet is gone
A prodigy in the art
For decades he wrote
With an unusual poetic spirt
With a proficiency scarcely equalled
Acclaimed as an unashamed patriot
A Welsh man to the core
An inspiration he was to many.

At a ripe old age
The inevitable happened
As the invincible claw pointed at him
In a twinkle the poetic giant fell
Fell never to write again.

Poverty

Poverty a contention
Creeping in allowed or disallowed
Its grip to establish
Spreading out its roots of misery
The nutrient to sap
Symbolising the lack that drains
The lack that the lacking
A paradox of life is.

Poverty segregates
Poverty delineates
Poverty creates a sharp line
A band of demarcation between humans
Between humans world wide.

In poverty were some conceived
In poverty were they nurtured
They sucked the breast of poverty
They were the products of poverty
And may yet be without hope.

Poverty varies in degree
Written boldly on the poor of poor
Can be perceived by the sensitive
The sensitive and the observant.

Poverty carries a stigma
Poverty can make one foolish
It constitutes immense damage
To the body, emotion and soul of the afflicted.
Poverty pushes
Pushes like a compelling force
The odd to do
Striving against will, the line to draw.
Left without an option
The plunge is taken
And the die is cast

Leaving the perplexity to unfold
Unfold, unfold, to unfold.

Crime Has No Colour

Crime has no colour
For a function of the heart is
Not of skin colour.

Man's heart is the same
And crime in man is the same
Diversity may differ
But each crime finds representation
Independent of race or ethnicity.

Crime has no colour
For it ensues of the abundance
The abundance of his heart
The heart, the inner man
The inner man, the true identity

Anger

Anger the devil's toll
His agent of manoeuvre
The agent in disguise
A root inscrutable
The complex of nature.

With it things built in a lifetime
Can be pulled down to ruins
Ruins beyond salvage
At the moment unguarded
It comes like a thief
The thief in the night.

The holy word says
"Be angry but sin not"
This is the balance
The balance of anger.

Even the masters
Can't master it
In a twinkle they are overtaken
Overtaken and besides themselves
In the afterthought they are taken aback
Taken aback they bemoan
But the seed is sown
And only blossom can.

By it the soul is devoured
The flesh is weakened
And energy ebbs away
Ebbs away like water down the stream
Flushing away joy and peace unhindered
The pieces difficult to reassemble.

The Battle of Life

We are all involved
Involved in the battle of life
Quietly or vehemently it rages
It rages nonetheless
Rages in all spheres of our life.

A battle diverse and profound
The battle for survival and importance
The battle to be heard and listened to
The battle for recognition and self actualization
The battle for respect and rights
The battle for riches and against poverty
The battle for freedom and against conscience
The battle for right and against wrong
The battle against ill-health and the vicissitudes of life
The battle against crime and the like
The battle against fear and foe
The battle against feeling and impulse.

The battle fields are widespread
Spreading all over
Ranging from the mind to the home
The work place and the streets
The realm spiritual and unseen
The court room of the learned judges
The battle rages
Only to cease
When the spirit departs the body
Departs, departs
Departs at the hour of fate.

The Human Mind

The human mind the seat
The seat of the personality
The personality on the throne
The throne of self government
Interacting with the world outside.

Some are great
Some are small
Others are mediocre
The human mind the seat
The seat of conceptions
Conceptions and desires
Noble or ignoble.

The mind is pliable
Highly elastic but breakable
The mind is insatiable
Equilibrium hardly achievable.

The great, the small and the mediocre are needful
Needful for a balance
The balance of mind set and of nature
That the universe at peace may be.

Mediocre minds glide
Glide along the surface of life
Leaving little print if any
On the sand of their time
After they are gone
It may not be apparent
Not apparent they passed
Passed through the path of life.

Great minds create
Great minds destroy
Great minds are achievers
Great minds inspire

But they perspire to inspire
Some were so ingenious
Others blessed with serendipity
They were ahead
Ahead of their time
And paid for it they did
On account of the divergence
The divergence of their mind.

Can't Have Your Way Always

No man however
However shrewd or prudent
However wise or foolish
However crafty or powerful
Can always
Always have things his own way.

Life is a process
One of give and take
Those seeking always to take
To take and their way to have
Selfish and unchecked.

May in the end lose more
Lose more than they would have given
For nature has a way
A balance to conserve.

Dreamland

As he laid his head on the pillow
He drifted adrift
Adrift to a land unknown
A land of a constellation of differences
A land of convergence and divergence
A land of the lost
A land of unveiling
The unveiling of the subconscious
A land of confusion and revelation
Revelation divine or mundane
A land of unreality.

Dreamland is the land
Where the conscious and the subconscious meet
Floating in the same plane
The inner self is revealed
Revealed to the outer self
The glimpse to catch of the inner man
Or of the hidden realm
The impalpable realm.

On waking
Awoken to reality
He began to analyse
Analysis and analysis of the analysis
In the end
He is not enlightened except
Except there is a light
A light of divine
Flashing from above or
Or flashing from within
From the unknown inner man.

Hatred

Hatred consumes
Consumes like consumption
Deep to the fabric it eats
The fabric of the body, soul and spirit
Leaving the victim empty
Empty like a cracked carcass
The true vitality gone.

When it burns
Red hot it drains
Drains the sap
The glittering to sustain
And in the process energy
Useful energy is wasted
Washed beyond recovery
The conservation law failing to hold.

It is easier to love than to hate
For the tree of hatred rooted
Drought resistant becomes
Flourishing branches to evolve
Ceasing to heed the farmer's bidding
Self sustaining, it ravages
The lamentation notwithstanding.

Nip it in the bud
That it flourishes not
For when full grown
At its mercy you are
Consuming and invading to the depth
It ravages the vitality to sap
To sap, to sap
Leaving no stone unturned.

Fear

Fear, as ancient as man
Common to all men
Common to all animals
Fear can be genuine
Fear can be morbid.

Genuine fear savours or saves
Morbid fear distresses
Percipients differ
Differing in the voyage of life
According to times
The times and seasons of life.

Fear causes flight
Inner or outer flight
The turbulence to quieten
But in fleeing from the source
You could be running into it
What a paradox
The paradox of fear.

Fear denied or hidden blossoms
Fear discussed melts
Times there are when
When fear is better confronted
Better confronted, better confronted
For then it ceases
Ceases fear to be.

The Human Face

The human face, the open mask
Revealing the man behind
As an inlet serving
Providing a clue.

The smile and the laughter
The grin and the frown
The blank and flat expression
The sad and weeping
The joy and the anger
The love and the hatred
The hangdog look of the culprit
The glittering face of a victor
And the dull look of a loser
All facilitated by the muscles
The muscles of facial expression.

Coded or mummified
It still expresses
Expresses the owner
For it is nature's decoder
Pretence notwithstanding.

We may hide the feeling
But the face
A true reflection still gives
For an open mask it is
The face is the open mask.

Technology

Technology a delight
An ease to mankind
Those advanced in her are blessed
The laggard, follow in the distance far
Being at the mercy.

Technology breeds technology
Technology breeds ingenuity
Technology breeds rivalry
Technology breeds a thriving economy
Technology breeds problems unforeseen
Technology breeds challenges daunting.

By it men
Have done the unthinkable
Achieving beyond conception
Breaking grounds untrodden.

An object of blessing
Blessing to humanity it has been
Saving and serving many
Easing life on the habited planet
On the other hand, it has been an instrument
An instrument of war, accident and devastation
Technology a delight
A succour ought always to be.

A Fool As A Prince

Born with a spoon
A silver spoon in his mouth
A prince ought to be wise
But foolish can be or become.

Groomed in luxury
Devoid of instruction
Service abounding
Pleasures unending
Grew up he did
A fool to become.

Born into it
Laboured not for it
Devoid of wisdom
He can't read
Neither the mood
Nor the times.

Consumed by passion
Refused to grow up
Bridled by appetite
His vision is obscured
And he can't see what they say
Ultimately he shall be ruled
Ruled by the servants
The servants he ought to rule.

True princes are not only born
They are also made
For nobility is not only to be craved
But also earned
A prince as a fool is a misnomer
A misnomer but a reality
An undeniable reality.

Tears From The Eyes

Tears from the eyes
It is for a cause
For yearnings unfulfilled
For yearnings unheard
For burdens that can't be shared
For dreams broken.

They find outlets in tears
An expression of deep seated emotion
Which for ages has been
Been the acquaintance of many.

And how sad!
For some, its sting will persist
Persist into everlasting
For others, the Almighty's hand will
Will their tears wipe away.

Tears can be sweet or bitter
Bitter tears abound
Sweet tears are few
But do tears have a cleansing?
They do I submit
I submit it does.

Thinking Astray About Thinking

He allowed his thoughts to drift
Drift and drifted away it did until
Until he began to think astray
Thinking astray and thinking aloud.

And he thought
Do plants think
Think they do he proposed
Or why are they sensitive?
Sensitive to light, touch and water
A reflex, he thought.
Could a reflex be a primitive form
A primitive form of thinking, he proposed.

To thinking astray there is no end
For analysis begets analysis
In the end, is there an answer?
Or are both thinker and thought lost?
Lost to incomprehensibility
In the realm beyond proof.

Body, Soul and Spirit

Man is a composite trio
Of body, soul and spirit
The body, the physical being
The soul, the seat of the mind
The spirit, the departing component
Departing at the hour of death.

The body, soul and spirit are inseparably bound
The soul joining the extremes
One affecting the other
In a fashion intricate
When they sing discordant tunes
Each pays the price
For they were fashioned
Fashioned to function in unison.

Racism A Canker

Racism a canker
A canker spreading like cancer
Spreading to poison
Poisoning the victim and the victor
Wherever it treads, it leaves traces
Traces of its malignity.

I sought it to justify
And I searched
Searched for a man purely human who
Who determined his birth place
Who self controlled when he was born
Who the architect was, of to whom he was born
Who had a say in his form
Who played a role in his origin
I sought earnestly the wide world
And none found
Thus concluded
Racism is unjustifiable.

Say you to me
I have not right
Right to pride myself in my origin
To pride myself in my fortune
To pride myself in my ethnicity
To pride myself in my colour
To pride myself in my form
To pride myself in my country
To pride myself in my parentage and heritage.

Of your right to pride
I deny you not.
But say I to you unmistakably
That the right to treat any other
Any other as subhuman
As subself on racial grounds, is not yours.
It is not yours

For you earned it not
And earn it can't
For but for the creator's design
It could have been you in the other
You in the other shoe.

Racism hidden or overt
In the high or low places
Wherever, it is trailed by a legacy.
A legacy of poor commentary
Ranging from devastation to ruin
From pogrom to war
From hatred to deprivation
From hunger to death
From rancour to mutilation
From prejudice to genocide
So despicable is it
That both the basis
And its end products
Are cankers
Cankers unjustifiable.
Turn thus from the canker
For in the end both can
Both the victim and the victor can be consumed.

The Strange Intruder

A stranger and an intruder indeed
A misguided man
A man with misguided intention
The self invited.

He comes crawling silently
Camouflaged for disguise
Using the cover of the dark hours
His intent to perfect.

With a heart full of mischief
And claws skilful in wickedness
Eyes penetrating and dreadful
Legs swift to carry to malignity
He performs his counsel
The counsel of his baleful heart.

After unleashing havoc
He retires in despair or praise
Waiting again for an opportuned moment.
When apprehended he turns the blame
Hidden from self, he can't see.

Love Turned Sour

When love turns sour
The lovers are bewildered
Amazed and frustrated
They question whether they were ever in love
Ever in true love
Having only old memories to treasure
They nurse the wound for .....

When love blossoms
The concealed is revealed
The blindness unstopped
And the real lover emerges
Emerges from the shadow
The shadow behind the veil
The always temporary veil.

When love goes sour
And the players give in
The romance melts
Melting like snow heated
The pieces crumble and the passion departs
Then only the divine hand
The allowed divine hand the pieces can pick up.

Man changes
And love does
Change appears the only thing permanent
The permanence of positive change in love
A function of grace and perseverance is.

Death The Caller

Death, death, death, oh death!
It comes calling
Calling the next victim
Fiercely or gently it comes
Swiftly or crawling
Calling at an hour untold
The spirit departs as closer it calls.

Think of it while it calleth not
For sure it will call
And you know not the hour
It is wise to prepare
Prepare for the inevitable caller.

For the transition can be sweet and welcome
The saved can yet rejoice
Rejoice at the glimpse of the caller
The caller unwanted
But we can't avoid.

Memories

Good and bad they abound
Trailing us like our footsteps
Imprinted in concrete
Failing sometimes to fade as we desire.

We relish the good ones
Wanting them ever green to remain
Nurtured and cuddled
A relief to provide
We love to wallow in their pools
Recounting them with great pleasure.

The bad ones are ravenous
Serving more as positive/ negative reinforcement
Hanging over like clouds of gloom
Entrapping us in the past of the past
Casting their ugly shadows wherever we go
Failing the cord to break.

Entrapped in them
We cast the blame
Refusing to be free
We are bound
Bound by the past to the past
Good or bad, progress is deterred
And we become the victim(s)
The first victim of our memories.

The Violent

Thank God they are few
Few rather than many
They feed on aggression like food
Violence fuels their life
They live on it or live by it
Modesty or sympathy is alien to them
For such they have no room
Violence is their joy
It is to them like water to a thirsty deer
Their victims at their mercy their pleasure.

As they maim and violate
They gain a feeling
A feeling indescribable
Best known only to them
Who stand as victors over their victims.

Aggression to them has become a way
A way of life
Slowly but surely
Violence their second nature became
Given to violence as a culture
No longer quietened otherwise.

They grew into it
Or were the product of it
Imbibed it or stumbled on it
For violence breeds violence
And violence begets violence

The cycle to perpetuate
Except at the turning point
Where the spirit rejuvenates
Relinquishing the past of old
The dark ugly past.

Hard Drugs

Drugs, drugs
Hard drugs
Leading into depths
Depths of precipitous decline
Where the victim can't see self
Nor commune with self
Engrossed in drugs
Nursing no other wish.

As if held in the claws
The claws of a mightier one
The shackles not easy
Not easy to disentangle from.
Held in the web of a cocoon
From which breakage is difficult
Caged by a gainless desire
The will is subsumed
Lacking the power to unlock
To unlock and be free.

Hard drugs, drugs hard
The yearning den that tears apart
Rips asunder the personality
Promising freedom
But yielding bondage
At the end of the road the person is lost
Lost to drugs, hard drugs
As another
Another of its countless victims.

Twisted Personalities

Twisted, twisted, twisted
Some are twisted personalities.
Twisted inside out
Negative or positive
They enjoy the twist or live with it.

Twisted in the head
Twisted in the mind and heart
Twisted in thinking
Twisted in spirit
Twisted in emotion.

Twisted in falsehood
Twisted in perversion
Twisted in passion
Twisted in joy and sadness
Twisted in argument.

A twisting not physical
The twist of twists
Revolving round an axis difficult
Difficult to discern
And to unknot.

The twisted a complex
Which to stretch forcefully is to break
Stretching devoid of the lubrication of will
Precipitating the crisis of crises.

Vengeance

it burns, it burns, it burns
It burns spreading like a wildfire to consume
Fuelled by anger and bitterness
Motivated by evil memories
Memories evil, not overcome by the forgiving spirit.

Vengeance rages
Rages like a bull out of control
Which no longer can be nursed to submission
The passion to take control now out of control
Burning it spreads
Bringing forth its offsprings.

The offspring of vengeance
The product of poisons
Poisons which spread the rampage
The whole entity to pervade
To pervade and to perverse.

Vengeance is like fighting fire with fire
In the end
No one is at peace
At peace, at peace, at peace
While the fires are stoked
Burn, burn, burn, they burn.

Vengeance is a wildfire
In the end it consumes
Showing no sympathy
And failing even to spare
To spare him who the fire lit
But burning all across its path

Ultimately the evil instrument turns
Turns against its users to devour
Devour, devour, vengeance devours.

Conscience

The silent court,
Of the impartial judge.
A habitat of truth unalloyed
An inner witness to truth.

When clear, as clear as water pure.
When fettered it is turbid
The turbidity apparent to self
Though obvious may not be to others.

The veil that unveils
Unveilng for self to see
To behold in truth
The picture hidden.

The quiet bell
Ringing aloud the truth.
The inner wall
Echoing aloud the undisputable
The deep well
From which oozes the waters of unbias.

We can argue loud
But understand we do
Its quiet voice of truth
We can put up a look
The contemptuous look of incorrigibility
An unrepentant look
But the conscience is unimpressed
Unimpressed and not deceived.
The trustworthy seat of truth

The seat of conviction and justification
A partner dependable, the true self partner
When not sealed as with iron
When not deluded as in the mad.

Believe In Yourself

Believe in yourself
For that is the pathway to greatness
Greatness and self actualization
Many are neither self nor others
Caught in the web of the undetermined
Floating in the common pool.

Refuse to be pushed around
Like a guided mule
Having no will or self say
Poured into the mould of others
Guzzling down the throat whatever is poured
Devoid of scrutiny and discernment
That the path of nobles is not.

Believe in yourself
Listen to the voice
To the voice of wisdom in others
But refuse to be teleguided
Teleguided and manipulated
Led where you know not
Led where you will not go.

Believe in yourself
And walk tall
With the inner head unbowed
Having the courage to say no when fit.
Take your stand
Stand on your conviction
For the weak are blown off as chaff

As dust by the storm
Not imparting their generation
The world passes them by
Their years counting not/nought.

Truth Is Unsoothing

Truth is unsoothing
Can be distasteful and hurtful
It upsets
But when accommodated it heals
For there is a balm in truth.

Truth not confronted willingly today
Confronts fiercely tomorrow
For truth though buried
Has a tendency to resurrect.

Truth is unsoothing
Lies are unsavoury
Lies are born twin
Lacking inner strength
Can't stand alone
Protecting the front
The rear is prone.

Truth though unsoothing
Stands self sufficient
Needing no support to thrive
For thrive it thrives alone
Even without followers.

Indulgence

Involved consciously
Or creeping in unwittingly
The cravers craving
Depths insatiable.

An exercise of lack of restraint
Restraint from the joy
The joy which the seed of sadness sows
Waxing and waning
Can't be fettered.

Slowly and steadily it grows
The embers may have been blown
Nursed unwittingly
The fire stoked
The indulgence spreads and grows
Taking root it is fortified
And axing it a difficult task becomes.

Indulgence is the sweetness that kills
Coming like thundering waves when blossom
Stoked it goes off in all directions
Burning like wild fire
Never satisfied
It is like chasing the wind
And never catching it.

Never catching the chase
The despair and pursuit continues
The vicious cycle unending

Except the compulsive fetter is broken
The binding fetters of indulgence
It never abates
Never abates, never abates.

Suffering

Suffering is the reality
The reality of living
The plight inevitable
The pain of a pill of grief.

While some refine us
Others crush
While some point to the direction
Others lead astray
Lead astray the circle to perpetuate.

Some suffering is wasted
Not allowed to yield the fruit
Their good fruit
Long after they are dead and gone
Their purposes vacuous remain.

Some suffering come on us
Come on us like vultures upon corpses
Hard to fathom
Difficult to ignore
Escape uncertain.
Sure to come as dew
As dew falling upon grasses on an autumn morning
Also they are sure to lift
As heat surely rises on a summer day
Like the seasons they come to pass
Can't last forever
When ripe like fruits
They fall off or wear off
The devastation settles
And the balmy season emerges.When it comes upon us
As pangs upon a woman
The woman in travail
We quake in terror
Put in disarray and dismay
We groan with eyes wet and hearts bleeding

Joy is at lowest ebb
As we seek the plight to turn around
Around to turn
Around to turn.

Risk

Risk is ever present
An ever present ingredient in human endeavours
May be obscured by mildness or gain
But risk perpetual remains.

There is risk in action and inaction
Ever present wherever in the universe
In the air, land or sea
It goes with us
Or stays with us
And it's reality we can't evade.

We can't evade
As we only exchange one for another
And risk an ever-present ingredient remains
Failing to bow to our dictates.

Solitude

Solitude, solitude
The quietness deafening
As if lone is a forest zone
Devoid of mortals save the stretch of trees
Trees and blades of grasses
As quiet as motionless.

Solitude, solitude
Born alone as if without a mother
Raised alone as if without a sibling
Raised alone like a loner
Died alone without sympathizers
Went in solitude to a quiet grave.

Devoid of fulfilment
Man feels lonely
Lonely though in a vast world
As though caged
Seeking escape from self.

As though in a web
Can't reach out
The loneliness to break
Can't escape from self
The loneliness to end.
Haunted by self
Can't run from his shadow
For wherever he goes
Close it stays
There being no divide
No divide from the darkness of solitude.

The Pressures of Life

From it none are immune
Tall or short
Plain or coloured they come
Never in want.

In their absence we feel
Feel empty and unchallenged
When present we are pressured
Pressured as though bursting.

Pressured beyond limit
And seeking escape
Some are led astray
Pressured astray into suicide
Hoping the darkness to end
But failing to see
To see that death is not a dead-end.

But suicide is
Is the end of a dark road
Only leading to further darkness
It is like a road that does not lead where it leads
The light of rest/peace
To such elusive remains.

Discouragement

The pathway of life is laden with it
The arch-enemy's weapon
The archer's potent missile
An arrow that has hurt many.

When courage is bid goodbye
Discouragement overflows
The man is overrun
Overrun and submerged
Vitality and passion are gone
And life an emptiness becomes.

In its moment a man must learn
Learn to pull himself by the boot straps
And stand
And stand in his inner man
For when a man stands in his inner man
Nothing can make him bow.

Stand up against the missile
For by it many have been
Been shot down and shut up
Their places in life rendered vacant
Gone before their time
Consigned to history books.

The discouraged are overcome
Overcome on the inside
Inner strength ebbed away
Can't stand without support
Clinging on as if by the thread
Which, the weight cannot support.

Be clothed in strength
Gain intestinal fortitude
Refuse to be crushed like trampled grass
Lest you be like them

Who in ignorance fell
Fell for the enemy's missile
Only to become their laughing stock
Weary and losing heart
Sifted beyond repair
Disentangled as dismembered.

The Eyes A Window

The eyes a window
A window into and out of
An expression of the inner man
Telling much about him
He who is hidden distant.

The eyes a well of life
But an expression of death can be
Expression overt or occult
Piercing through the thick cloud of darkness
The silence to break.

In conceal it deceives
The unanalytical beholder taken in
Failing to see through the window
The small aperture window
He is taken aback.

With the eyes, mind and spirit open
You see through the window
Clear as in daylight
The real is preserved
The shades are obliterated
And the eyes a true window becomes.

Disease

It creeps in like a crab
To darken the doorstep where it docks
At an hour untold
And at a moment unexpected.

Manifesting itself in a gamut
The gamut of symptoms and signs
Signs discernable by the learned
Though elusive can be.

Disease afflicts
Neither respecting the poor nor the rich
It transcends barriers
Cutting across sex and social class
Across race and culture
Unlimited by age and belief.

None are immune
Immune from its savagery
Save for grace.
It comes as a guest
Invited or otherwise
It establishes its abode
Oblivious of the victim's wish.

The victim's wish, the victim's wish
One not relishable
About man's arch-enemy.
A world without disease
Lies only in the world of imagination
Far out of reach
Not within human bounds.

Boomerang

It always returns
The good or the bad
Grows and comes back to us
The circle to complete
To complete like a boomerang.

Our action or speech grow
Grow from a foothold to a stronghold
Unshakable they remain
Remain and boomerang.

The good or the bad never die
They only lie in wait
Waiting to boomerang
May be at a moment forgotten
When the memory kindle can't.

Erasure difficult
As though written
Written with diamond pencil
Or with a pen of iron
Linger they do
Long or short
As if in suspense
Waiting only to boomerang.

What we sow, we reap
The good or the bad
Comes in search of the sower
Knowing where it came from
Knows where to go
Boomerang, boomerang, to boomerang.

However improbable or enigmatic
However ironic or subtle
The boomerang returns
We may know not how

How the path is traced
But sure return it does
The circle to complete.

We love to sow
But men hate
Hate to see the fruit
The fruit of his wrongdoings
But inevitably it boomerangs
Boomerang, boomerang, it boomerangs.

No Perfection

Man is created perfect
But man himself is imperfect
And man's handiwork imperfect likewise
For he is limited.

Man is limited
His limit is limitless
Being limited in all spheres
And perfection in man
An illusion remains
For infallible he is not
In man there is thus no perfection.

Complex Variables

Many variables determine
Determine the outcome of events
Events in human endeavours
Complex variables they are
Or varying complexes
Forming an intertwined network
Whose facets are boundless
Creeping on each other
Difficult to disentangle.

Some variables are active
Others passive
Some predominant
Others are recessive.

An outcome is a product
The product of an interplay of complex variables
Merging and fusing
The boundaries are obscure
The accessories may become the dominant
The trigger to fire.

With the die cast
We can only speculate
What variables were operative
But complex variables they are
Intertwined in a complex fashion
Their interaction beyond complete discerning.

Believe in the Future

Believe, believe, I believe in the future
The yesteryears we can't salvage
The future lies in the belief of today
Believe in the future
For thereby can it be redeemed.

To refuse to believe is to negate
To negate the prospect of hope
The good hope which only the future
Only the future holds.

To cease to believe is to flush
Flush down the drain as waste
That which is yet to be
Left for salvaging.

The light of yesterday may have been put off
The light of today may be dim
But the light of tomorrow is for the kindling
By believing in the future
We choose for the light to glow
And glow it can
Can glow, can glow.

Arrogance

The arrogant is full
Full of himself
Though empty he may be
Lacking real substance.

The arrogance of some is
Is breathtaking
Breathtaking and mind boggling
Being grossly short
Short of sound reasoning.

Those who go down its pathway
In the ultimate are forced to
Forced to swallow their pride
Humbled and humiliated
Having nowhere to turn
Their ego deflated
They lie subsumed.

The product of a misguidedness
Nurtured in the subconscious
Rising to the surface
The plum buds
Fanning out the thorny petals
The petals now difficult to prune
Difficult to prune.

The Arm of the Law

The arm of the law
At various times may appear
Appear long, short or non-existent
Appear too harsh or too weak.

The arm of the law ought
Ought to be the arm of justice
Straight and open
But at times it is crooked and clenched.

It then becomes
The arm aiding and abetting
Under the guise
The guise of legal technicalities
The good is advanced
While the real reason is obscured
But the truth, the truth remains.

For though the guilty may escape
Escape in the court of law
He can't escape in the court of conscience
From which he can neither hide
Nor be declared free
There the arm of the law is strong
Very strong, straight and open
And only the truth sets free
The naked truth, devoid of colouring.

My Love Insect

The butterfly my love insect
One elegant and adorable
Enveloped in beauty
Endowed with it by the maker.

It zooms in
In with a soft elegance
And in quietness it exits
Exits against anticipation
Going where the nectar calls.

Colourful in amazement
Variegated in degrees uncountable
It is an attraction
An attraction to all.

An insect beautifully harmless
As it flaps its wings
Its colours to spread
Gliding mildly in the air
We can see it is at peace
At peace with nature.

A Ray Of Hope

Hoping against hopelessness
In the midst of darkness and despair
Stretching forth to see
A ray of hope to behold
And a glimpse of it faintly catching.

Sinking as in a mire
Seeking a hand to see
Stretched forth to save
To deliver from the uncertainty
A gloomy future paints.

Painted in black and tinges of yellow
Tinges of yellow as a ray
The blue rousing like rivers
Like rivers of water the dark to dispel.

From the flood, comes a ray
And where there is a ray
A ray of hope
There can be a flood
A flood of hope can be
Can be for you.

The Limiting Factor

Is man born free?
Or limited inherently or by personal design
Almost all have personal limitations
Limitations limiting.

The best we can be
The best we ought to be
Is truncated
Truncated by limitations
Limitation needing outgrowing.

Limitation diverse
Diverse as diverse
As diverse as man
As diverse as fingerprints.

Superficial or deep
Occult or overt
Manifest to self, hidden to others or
Manifest to others hidden from self
Wherever it buds, the limitation hinders.

Hinders from the best
The best we were made to be
Made to be
Made to be.

The Sun

The sun, the sun
A universal natural force
Arising in dazzling brilliance
Clothed with beauty and power
At noon time
In full strength it exudes
Exuding power and glory
A power and glory the naked eye can not
Can not confront but
But can behold
We also joy as we bask
Basking in its warmth
In the evening tide
It settles with a glorious quietness
And gentle radiance.

It rules in strength
Over the day
Over the day
As ordained by the Lord
The Lord of the universe.

How life on earth depends
Depends largely on it
With its light we are blessed
Saved from darkness and stumbling
We walk the day
Seemingly unconscious of the ruler
The sun a ruler in its own right.

Sentiment

Sentiment a bait for the unobjective
By it logic is forced to
Forced to stand on its head
Finding expression
In no other way.

Sentiment my resentment
For its catalogue of failures
Failure to identify the issue
Failure to address the issue
In its stead emotions are played
And the issue unresolved remains.

Fall not for the bait
For there is a nobler way to tow
The path of honour undeterred
Of objectivity unalloyed
Of the lines of divide drawn
Drawn even when it hurts
For that is the path of the nobles.

Emotions are rich
Rich and diverse
Meant to be expressed
But the line of divide
Yet must be drawn
Drawn between sound reasoning and sentiment
Between logic and tinted emotion
That temporarily satisfies
Satisfies only passion
The passion by which not a few
But many are afflicted.

Habits

Habit forming is human
They grow on us
Or we grow on them
Good or bad the choice we make
But ultimately the choice makes us.

The bad habits are easy to cultivate
The good ones difficult to form
When formed and casted
They are hard
Hard to change
Hard to change.

The bad ones bridle
Bridle to the point of slavery
May have been nurtured in innocence
Full blown it grows
Grows a death knell to become.

Many there are
Who live in the shallow grave of life
The shallow grave of bad habits
Entrapped in the mire
They are bowed inside
Being distraught, they struggle
Struggling against self
Deeper they may sink
And the seed is sown
The seed of early death.

The good ones not as effortless
But shine they do
They are like the balm of life
And yield their dividend in the ultimate.

The Colour Of Justice

What is the colour of justice?
To different people, justice means different things
And the colour of justice appears
Appears to be dependent
Dependent upon the perceivers eyes.

Is justice white?
Blue, yellow, black or red.
White depicting right standing
Blue symbolising love, protection, care and tenderness
Yellow a reflection of light
The light of truth
Black typifies the cover of darkness
The cover under which malignity prevails
Red attributable to the blood flowing
Flowing and crying for justice.

Or is justice a mixture of colours?!
And what you see depends on where you look
The victim says it is white
The culprit says it is blue
The lawyer says it is black
The judge says it is yellow
And the onlooker says it's red.

In the ideal world
The colour is justice is
Is singular
It is the colour of truth proven
Truth proven and stood for

That is the true colour of justice
And truth is independent
Standing dignified in it is own right
Justice, justice, justice
Has only one colour.

The Crafty Politician

By and large the responsible ones are gone
Gone to the grave or lost to despair
Searching through the globe
The responsible and faithful are sparse
And the 'nobles' have turned crafty.

Prior to election he comes prowling
Assured his fate lies with them
Even the fastidious are impressed
He pays the price
Nursing his hidden agenda.

After win, the mask is unveiled.
The egotism emerges
He becomes the epitome
The epitome of deceit and conceit.

In time, with time
He becomes a repository of infallible wisdom
Priding in policies
Rather than in care of the subjects.

He promised glare
But delivers gloom
A hireling to the core is he
Devoid of the shepherd's spirit
The shepherd's good spirit.

A Day in Winter

Out I came into the cold
The cold embrace of a snowy day
The streets white
The houses plastered
And the roofs covered
The green grasses turned white
And the shedding trees frosted.

As I walked the white slippery path
I felt an unusual freeze
My teeth gnashing
The hairs were raised
The eyes tearing
And my breath smoking.

In my misery
I looked above
As if asking
Why the creator
Created snow.

Snow is white pure
Typifying the maker
Who the seasons control
Snow is beautiful and inviting
But deadly can be
Snow is a witness to winter.

Have A Dream

Have a dream
Have a dream
For our dreams make us in the ultimate
As in dreaming we are projected
Launched by the power of a dream
Into the trajectory of achievement.

We can, we can
We can dream and not achieve
But we can hardly achieve without dreaming
For achievers are dreamers.

A dream compels
compels to propel
To propel into great achievements
For dreams are the place of define
The defining place for achievements.

When a dream is born
An achievement is conceived
If nurtured both blossom
Maturing they grow into manhood.

In failing to dream
We deny ourselves the joy
Deny the joy of seeing
Seeing a dream come true.
Deny the exhilaration of the metamorphosis
As out of the shadows of dreams comes reality.

I know I know

I know I know
I know I know that I know
But what I know I can't prove
It is a knowing of faith.

I know not how I know
But I know I know
I am persuaded I know
Know above conviction.

A knowing impalpable
A knowing beyond the sense of sensing
In realms unnatural
Where the senses can't make sense of
And faith is let loose.

Faith is let loose
Let loose let loose
And on the run to catch
To catch the supernatural
And to make real the real.

Disappointments

We desire them not
But happen they do day to day
Being powerless we watch
For it was not for us to appoint.

Not for us to appoint
Lest we would have
And there would be no need
Need for disappointments.

In its hour
Expectations are aborted
Hopes are withdrawn
Drifting away as dark clouds dispelled.
The look is vacant
The disquiet loud
And confidence is blown
Blown apart like seeds by the wind
Such seeds knowing not the soil
The soil on which they would land.

But in the appointed time
Disappointments cease
Cease like a dream ending
Ending for another to unfold
For the dream whose time has come
No man, no man can resist
And happen it will.

The Contrasting Veils

The world, a world of inexplicable contrast.
Where some are lacking and starving
While others are swimming in affluence inestimable
Only experience can tell
The mind cannot fully conceive
Neither can words adequately describe
The agony due to lack
The trauma difficult to manage.

Some have never seen beauty
Lacking natural beauty
And surrounded by the ugly.
On the contrary, some have only beauty seen
Of all kinds and dimensions.

Contrast in the same world
Like two contrasting sides of the same coin
A contrast world wide.
One that has come to stay
Emerging from time immemorial
And biting hard on imagination.

Midnight Hour of Life

In the midnight hour of life
There in the midst of darkness
The silence is pervading
But the turmoil loud and deafening
The constitution is in turmoil.

In turmoil but can't run
Can't run for fear of fall
And can't stop for fear of the haunting
The haunting darkness
With the ensuing confusion.

The brain is confused
In a state of logical disjunction
Shrivel as though empty
Bursting as though overflowing
It is like being in a straight jacket
To bend is to crack.

The midnight hour is
Is the hour of trial and travail
Those we wish we don't have to
Have to confront
But they come and pass
For the daylight to emerge.

To emerge like a dangling rose
Waiting to be plucked
Picked and taken advantage of
This is the mystery of darkness
For out of your midnight hour
Can come your rose for the picking.

Late Wishes

We all have them
In varying degrees
Late wishes
Or good wishes coming too late
As good as buried can do no good.

With the benefit
The benefit of hindsight
We wished we acted
Acted very differently
But such wishes too late are
For the die is cast.

The rubicon is crossed
And late wishes can't overturn
Can't overturn the havoc
For too late they came
Thus are condemned
Condemned to the grave
And thrive can't.

Weak wishes ultimately become late
For they are weak
And no good can do
Tied by the fetters of weakness
Can't rise against the odds
Failing to gain strength
In the end they are turned late
Late, late, consigned to the grave.

Empty

Empty, empty, empty.
An emptiness perturbing
Such is the emptiness of man
As empty as a barrel empty.

Came empty
Departed empty
At birth unconscious of asset
At death can't take a penny/cent.

In the conscious life largely empty
For only but a few
A few find the narrow path
The path to the fullness of fulfilment
A full of fullness absent in many.

Struggling against conviction
In contention always
For there is a vacuum in man
Which always remains empty
And nothing else can fill
Save the fitting key
Which the emptiness unlocks
Denial can't and doesn't
Can't fill the empty emptiness of man.

The Songs of Birds

As I reclined
Reclined in the lonely countryside
I heard the songs
The songs of birds.

The songs, songs
Echoing clear
From the proximate forest
The sweet songs entrancing
Entrancing and disarming.

The language I can't fathom
But the appeal I cannot resist
Can neither resist nor deny
Songs natural natural
Only nature can give.

Food

Food our sustainer
The source of our physical strength
As varied as nature
From culture to culture
The choice meal differ.

We despise/ignore it to our peril
We overindulge in it to our destruction
A destruction unwitting
Nonetheless abides and abounds.

Food our nourishment
Giving vitality to our cells
Without it we are limited
By it we are enhanced
In its balance we are secure(d).

A rallying point it is
The rallying point of culture and rituals
Its importance bellowed
As the indispensable ingredient
Necessary for man's survival.

Noise

Noise the unsynchronised decibel
Tones unbalanced
The like of some
The dislike of others.

An irritation to many
A distracting influence
The means to attention seeking
The bane of sound intellectual output.

Unlike music
Lacking rhythm
Can't make sense.
Bashing and cracking
Lacking harmony
Amounting only to the voice of confusion.

Noise can be powerful
Impulsively maddening and intrusive
The banging and the smashing
Lacking inspiration.

Doubly vacuous
The product of distorted orientation
Satisfies not
Save the disturber
And in scaring a foe.

Voice of Bias

The good listener hears it often
Present always
Echoing loud and clear
Though subtle can be.

In the high street
And in the low corners
Following where sentiment and prejudice leads
Blind to objectivity.

Even the Courts
The Courts of law are riddled with it
Though the habitat of truth ought to be
The voice of bias
The voice of falsehood tinted.

Lazy Brats

If the cap fits you wear it
Lazy brats they are
They run to cash the wage
But they foot drag to do the work.

They sow in laziness
But want to reap the fruit of diligence
Lazy brats they are
Lacking personal work ethics
And having no commitment to duty.

They love pleasure
But despise work
They are blind to the link
Stretching their legs before they are seated
End up falling like tumbling rock
And like a rolling stone
Gather no substance
For lazy brats they are.

Failures

The acquaintance of many
Failures or the prospect of it
Though despised
We see from day to day
They seem characteristic of the difficult subject
The difficult subject life is.

The greatest of failures
Is failure with God
Or inner failure
Leading down the drain
The drain of further failure.

Failure with God leads to misery
Misery and eternal defeat
Separation from the hope of hopes
Beyond the realm of advocations.

Inner failure comes from a crushed spirit
Crushed and crumbling
Crumbling and crumpled
Lacking strength in the inner man
The heart is bowed
Struggling to rise from the challenging heap
The heap of ruins failure connotes.

Failure though we detest
An ugly ducking can turn
A blessing in disguise
Leading where we otherwise will not get to.
As in rising to the challenge
A glory is released to blossom

Fanning out like the petals of beautiful flowers
In whose beauty we can bask
Basking to refresh from the wounds
The wounds failure inflict.

Imagination

Wide as wide
Wide and wild
As wide as boundless
Devoid of elastic limit
Stretching as far as we can go.

What we can imagine
We can become
What we can imagine
A possibility becomes.

Imagination unveils for us
Granting us a passage
A passage into the realm of possibilities
Where the inhibitions are inhibited
And a leeway into achievement is created.

Imagination also can inhibit
Unveiling to us a foe
A foe and fear unreal
Lying only in the realm of conception
Deferring from the plunge to take
The plunge of the villain.

Imagination at times can run riot
Flying ahead of the victim
It is like a man running
Running ahead of himself
Or against himself
And breaking the rules.
The sieve can't hold water
And containment an impossibility becomes.

Imagination is the creator's weapon
Hooked to it as to a prong
Versatile becomes in creativity
Exploring with skill

The hidden to unearth
To unearth and to unmask.

Were He Not Born

Were he not born
What would it have been like?
Would he have had the joy?
The joy of being unborn
Unborn into a world of strife.

The world, a world of strife.
Strife and never ending struggle
Spiritual, emotional, socioeconomic and physical strife
A struggle ignited with the first breath
But may by the last not terminated
So is the struggle of mankind
Who blossoms but for a while.

Man and the Environment

The environment our dwelling
Varying as the creator dictates
Can be clement or hostile
When clement it soothes
When hostile it bites.

When clement and balmy
Man is illusioned
And thinks he is in control
Absolutely in control.

When biting hard, it comes.
Comes in a twinkle
In a twinkle with devastation
The devastation that melts
Foiling everything in its path
As helpless we watch
It reminds us of our humanity
Humans with limitations.

From the quaking earth to the flooding zone
The tornado, cyclone and the gale
The active volcano with its molten lava
The wildfire; the red devil.
The sliding ground leading under
The mudslide burying alive
The snowy trap of the winter day
The stroking heat of the desert land
The environment our dwelling
We can only try not to worsen.

Not Meant To Be

Man aspires and envisions
But not all are meant to be
To be what they earnestly desire
Determination however profound
Can all not catch
From the well of achievement
As man follows the path ordained.

Think large and plan big
For that your prerogative is
But when hopes are dashed
And dreams broken
Have the grace to stand
Not by all means desiring
For some are not meant to be
Not meant to be
To be what they want.

For however far they come
Coming close
Close in the road of achievement
In the final analysis
The goal eludes
Eludes like a bird
Like a bird fleeing a snare
For they were not meant to be.

Blossoming At Night

Some blossom at night
Blossoming at the night time of life
A product of patient perseverance
Persevering until they see
See the star smile
The stars and the sun smile on them
And their flowers nerved, unveil.
Unveil their beauty
For all to see.

But they have toiled
From morning, through noon to night.
And now the moon is full
Full for them to joy in.

Their riches coming at night
Blossom remains
Remaining until the departing hour
The hour of fate.
But a good legacy they leave
Going onto yonder, somewhat fulfilled
Blossom they have at night.

God Near or Far

At times the Lord is so near
He seems as near as within
At other times, he is further than far away
He seems to have forsaken
I am in a strait betwixt two
To believe or to doubt.

He seems to me to care
To care, to care less
Less than his holy word portend
I trusted, but succour yet seems far.

I find no balance in my snare
The snare of the reality of his reality
And the reality of my realities.
The snares from which there is no hiding place
Oh wretched man that I am
Where lays comfort.

In my despair
I looked up
And found succour
Succour in a reflection of his word
Saying walk not by sight
But by faith.

Thus the reality of his friendship kindles
Kindles and rekindles
Rekindles and glows.
Now know I that Jesus is a friend
One closer than a brother
And herein is the place of rest
Rest quiet rest.

Reflection

Reflection a moment
A moment of self communion
Self communion and self appraisal
Dialoguing with self
Seeing beyond the inversion in the mirror
The true picture to perceive.

There are times in life
When we ought to
To sit down with self
And take the stock
The stock of our lives
Devoid of prejudice and self pity
An appraisal deep and sincere
The weeds to root out
And the foxes to expel.

Reflection on the bad, the good and the ugly
The essence of life to kindle
The husband, the wife
The father, the mother
The son, the daughter
The brother, the sister
The friend, the foe
The worker, the player
The influence, the havoc
We have been
Been in the path of life.
The reflection we ought to heed
When the curtain is not drawn
And lifes table is still spread before us.
A reflection deep and sober
Profound and diverse
Digging to unearth the real
That the gems might shine
And the flowers blossom
For the gems and the flowers in each reside

Waiting to wax
To wax and to glow.

The Crafty Man

The crafty man the crooked and foxy
A personification of deceit in and out
Cunning is second nature to him
Respect for truth alien.

He winkles to slay
He giggles to perverse
He gesticulates to seduce
Gimmickry is his talent
He breaths deceit as a norm
Blatant dishonesty is his trade.

He Had Not A Home

Home a place of rest and relief
Home a source of courage and comfort
But alas he had not a home
He lived in houses
But had not a home.

In anguish he searched for a home
His effort without fruition
He then reclined and declined
Settling for a no home living
But hoping against hope
He hopes a home to build
Or the likeness of it.

A home is built
Built on love and care
Integrity and selflessness
Many have not a home
But have houses
Houses with human dwellers
With such it's like an empty lifetime.

Seek a home to build
Building a home is not
Not building structures
It is building relationships
Relationships that exist within a structure
Seek thus a home to build
A place of rest and comfort.

Change

Change a confronting reality
The times of our lives change
Reflecting the uncertainties in which man is enmeshed
Positive change is desirable
The prospect of negative change torments.

I have seen the poor become rich
And the wealth of the rich collapse
Collapsing like a pack of cards.
I have seen the frail become strong
The dying become healthy
And the healthy cut off like chaff.

I have seen the wise become foolish
And the foolish become wise
The prisoner turned president
And the ignoble gaining nobility
While the prince is reduced to a refugee.

I have also seen
The sinner turned new
And the saint blemished
The barren blossom
And the servant having his way
The brink of collapse mended
And the strong brought down.
Some changes defy belief but
But true changes they are.

Some are distraught at the prospect of change
Positive or negative change
They are distraught and perturbed
Seeking to know what the centre holds. They could miss
the mark

Miss the mark and miss the point
And the object of change remains
Remains elusive
And elusive remains.

Veil Upon The Heart

There is a veil
A veil serving as a frontlet
On everyman's heart
Heart not physical
But the heart, the inner man.

The natural man's heart is full
Full of deception unspeakable
And of vices untold
That even his good is covert
Covert in comparison
And evidences of it abound
Abound for all to see.

The veil upon the heart
Can be removed only
Only by circumcision
Circumcision by regeneration
For that is the pathway ordained
Ordained by him
Him who the heart created.

Governed By What?

Man loves to think he is free
Free absolutely free
But in reality
He is governed
Governed by what he can't disentangle from.

Each man is governed
Governed by things varied
From spiritual through the mundane to the despicable.
Each man is governed
Consciously or unconsciously governed.

By what are you governed?
Governed by God supreme
Or by religion without life
Governed by morals or by immortality
Governed by fear or by mysticism
Governed by intellect or by irrationality
Governed by habits old or by mortal role models
Governed by money or by work
Governed by righteousness or by sin
Governed by power or by weakness.

Man can't be absolutely free
For in being governed by freedom
He is bound by freedom
And free free he can't be.

Psychological Nourishment

All mortals need it
The nourishment non physical but tangible
Basking in a sunshine devoid of it
Swimming in a milieu unsavoury
We become prone
Prone to neurosis or psychosis
Where the stretch has snapped.

Swimming in the pool of its lubrication
We stay afloat
In the sanity zone
Getting the push and the kick we need
Motivated to strive ahead
The battles of life to win.

The nutrients as variable as food
From the spiritual to the mundane
The deep to the superfluous
The job satisfaction and the good relationship
The power wielded and the riches possessed
The success of pursuits and the dreams come true
And the elation of conscious usefulness
Like the positive reinforcing the positive
To grant us the sleep of psychological satisfaction.

The words of encouragement lifting up
Lifting up the spirit from the dungeon
Bringing out from the well of despair
The love like rivers of water flowing
Flowing, flowing to heal.
At other times
The misty eyes of the evil day
Tend to soothe
Serving as a positive negative.

In the absence of psychological nourishment
Psychochemical disjunction supervenes

It is as though the falcon ceases to hear the falconer.
The discordant tunes echo
And pain is let loss
In the river of the mind
Surging through, the gate is broken
And the ripples apparent becomes to all.

The Hospital

The hospital a busy site
A site of atmospheric diversity
Ranging from passion to fear
From joy to agony
From despair to complacency
From apathy to withdrawal.

The impatient patient comes
In trust and distrust
Seeking an answer
To his plight and plaque.

The sick comes
Dull and anxious looking
Hoping against the odds
Looking unto the care provider as a saviour
Though he be not the author of life.

Dying Before Their Time

They were long gone before they are gone
Working their fingers to bone
Obsessed or possessed by work
The balance they lack
And slipped they did
Slowly but surely
Crossing the line of divide.

Hard work is good
Hard work is commendable
But to work harder than hard is imbalance
Imbalance and want of wisdom
Sooner or later his strength ebbs away
For nature abhors
Abhors imbalance.

The riches he sought
But has no time to joy in
Even his dog resents his absence
The spouse and children at the mercy of work
Good as dead
For he was gone
Gone before his time.

Man A Complex

Man is a complex
A being body, soul and spirit
Where the trio are inextricably bound
Occurring as a complex interweave.

Man is a complex
A physical wonder
In which the systems
Are detached but intertwined
Forming an entity unique.

The nervous system, a complex network.
The heart, a marvellous engine.
The vascular system, an unbroken channel.
The respiratory system, as the life with the outside world.
The abdominals, the untiring firehouse.
The kidney, a credible clearing agent.
The limbs, our great support.
The reproductives, our source of life.
The sensories, the inlets and the outlets.
The skin, a sensitive limiting membrane;
Obscuring the inner man.

All are bound
Working in synchrony
According to the designer template
Words and science fail
Fail us to explain in totality
The intricate working of the being called man
For man a complex truly is.

She Knew Not She Had It

Briskly she ran back to have it
And then returned to her path
Later it came pouring
Pouring like a flush
Burdened and perturbed
Drenched and dripping
She lamented
But knew not she had it.

Then in a drift she saw
She saw her choice colour
A red umbrella it was
The most needed for the hour
But she knew not she had it.

Thus is the riddle of life on occasions
We seek an answer from afar
While close to us it is
Knowing not we had it.

The Wind

The wind a natural phenomenon
Hovering to and fro as ordained
As ordained by the creator of nature.
A phenomenon we can't see
But we can feel
One we can't see
But is undeniable.

The wind a force
One we can neither contain
Nor curtail
As it blows at the command
The command we can't hear
But the whistling can perceive
As across it blows.

It comes blowing
Needing no right of way
When gently it comes, it soothes.
When it comes gusting, it is fierce and damaging.
It comes blowing down, up or off
The things in its mapped path
It ravages in a twinkle
Leaving us only the tales to tell.

The Quaking Earth

Suddenly it quakes
In a twinkle the devastation is unleashed
At an hour untold
In the zone prone or unprone.

When it strikes
Helter skelter we run in the proximate sites
Running for open shelter
We hope in apprehension
For a quiet settlement.

In the aftermath
As the shocks supervene
And the Richter we tell
Ranging from instrumental through ruinous to catastrophic
Perplexed we unpill the ruins
Unpill to rescue
And the death toll to count.

As we grief in despair
We are reminded
Reminded of our humanity
Humans we are
Not almighty
And the quaking earth
We can't stop
We can't stop.

In A Vast Landscape

Out I came in a distant countryside
Sighting a vast landscape
I was thrilled
For here nature is at peace
At peace, being sparsely populated.

On a summer day
Out of the farmhouse
As I lifted my eyes the beauty to behold
Coming to sight was the green grass
The green grass on the undulating plane
Reflecting in variation the sunlight.

As further I moved in the overgrown thickets
Came the lush forest zone
Trees big and tall
With branches swaying as the wind commands
Branches dangling with fruits variegated
Also the trees fallen but rooted
Refusing yet to give up.

Further in the forest
Came the hills and the valleys
And the water falling
Falling on rocky platforms
The turbulence to quieten.

The beauty of the landscape
My soul quieten
Bringing on me an unusual serenity
A serenity with pleasure inexplicable
Nature is kind, such landscapes us to give.

Flowers

Flowers a beauty to behold
A beauty natural and profound
A beauty enticing and captivating
A beauty even the despiser cannot resist.

They radiate quiet beauty and sweet fragrance
In the fragrance of their smell
And the fragrance of their look
The beholder is bemused
Bemused by the innocuous elegance they portray.

Flowers a symbol
The symbol of love
As it we exchange
The love sparkles
Sparkles the hidden words to echo
The echo revibrating as through its petals we look.

Flowers are nature's quiet echo
The echo of beauty and love
The echo of sweet fragrance and gentleness
The echo of invitation and wantedness
The echo of serenity and passion
Passion, good passion
Which words fail us expression to find for
Flowers, nature's way of echoing volumes.

The Aeroplane

The aeroplane
In the port it stands
Having pride of place
Then smoothly and gently it goes
Goes through the run-way.

Soon it glides
Swiftly and elegantly into the sky
Roaring as it goes
Gliding like a bird
Like a bird in the air.

A reflection of wizardry
The manufacturers wizardry
Delicate but full of strength
An invention unique
The work of a master craft.

Blazing through the sky
The novice is bemused
Wondering about the ease
It's easy sustainability in air
To rest his case
He concludes it is a product
The product of avid scholarship.

In My Distress

I now know sorrow
Like he that never knew joy
My heart aches
And I am utterly disquieted
My bones roar in silent vehemence
For deep psychological pain
And my zeal melts away like snow
Vanishing like grass consumed by fire in the harmattan.

There remains not strength in me
My flesh is like that of the down trodden
Unto who else can I look
Save the God of my salvation
Waiting in faith for the promise.

The Age Of Wisdom

As a man grows
There is a time to come of age
A time to grow up unto manhood
Leaving behind the pellets of immaturity.

At the age of wisdom
He combines firmness with gentleness
Love with discipline
Restraint with patience
Maintaining a delicate balance
The balance between sentiment, passion and
objectivity.

The issues of life he weighs better
Looking with insight and outsight
The crisis of life to resolve
As he treads the latter path.

If by the age of wisdom
A man a fool remains
He is likely so to forever
For only few lessons can
Can be learnt thereafter
But is the age of proper application
Application of the lessons of life
Building then on the foundation
For a man ought to grow
Growing into manhood an imperative is.

The Battle Never To Be Won

There is a battle that never can be won
It is the battle against conscience
The battle may rage wild and flame high
It could be as a quiet inner turbulence
A flame unquenchable
Uncalmable otherwise
Only to be calmed
By submission or defeat.

We may deny it
But the conscience cannot be silenced
In the quiet hour it ripples
It ripples, springing like a board
The spring unstoppable
Time and time may erode
Erode the vehemence of battle
But the battle is unwon
Unwon eternally.

The Prolific Writer

The prolific writer, the uncurtailable
And the heavily burdened.
He writes with a profundity hardly to be equalled
Expressing the riches of his mind.

His pen is a highly potent weapon
A weapon of pen-warfare
Combining great intellect with inspirational drive
He writes and rewrites
His write up distinctive and appealing.

Drawing out the conscience
Dragging out the subconscious
Calling attention to hidden treasures
Treasures unseen
Laying in veiled bodies
Needing to be unearthed.

Moonlight

The moonlight a delight
It arises in the heavenlies
In quietude and splendour
The night light for us to give.

Full moon a delight
The lovers delight
For in its quiet brightness
They can caress
Caress in the serenity and safety it provides.

The moonlight a delight
A delight for children
An opportunity for fun and play
Under its guide they play
play their dreams into reality
Or their reality into dreams.

Moonlight a concern
A concern to the mischievous
Whose malignity it unveils
When full blown
Giving no cover for their acts of darkness
For its candelas though low, they can't confront
They can't confront it.

Seeking Rest

The essence of life is hidden
The heart always thirsting
A state of permanent equilibrium is never reached.
At times life does not
Does not worth the importance attached to it
The crucial issue is the salvation
The salvation of one's soul.

For in salvation
Lays rest
Rest true rest
Rest for the precious soul
Soul so precious
Weighing more than the world whole
So precious is the soul of man
Man made in his image.

The Young Man's Confusion

His heart in a state
A state of confusion and mixed feeling
Under the burden
Burden of desire to live up to expectation
He yearns helplessly in despair and dismay.

Confused as to whether to please self
To please self or to please God
To please God or to please others
To please God or to please his impulse
To please God or to please reality.

The reality of his state
A state from which there is not easy escape
A state of passion, vision, mission and imagery
A state of disequilibrium
A state of disconsonance
Where the falcon cannot
Cannot hear the falconer.

But yet he sees
Sees in the midst of these
A ray
A ray of hope in prayer and diligence
And herein finds he a fortress.

The Beggar

Standing at the post
Or wandering around
He (she) pleads for alms
Expecting in despair.

With heads raised on the outside
But bowed on the inside
They plead their way
In desperation or anger.

The product of poverty
Poverty and depravity
Begging to feed
To feed the hunger within
And the thirst to satisfy.

Forced to it
Or chosen by it
Begging a lifestyle becomes
Entrapped they continue
The pleasure or the hurt
Theirs become
And thus persist.

The Contradiction Of Joy

Joy, joy, joy
The sight of the site of joy
Is not without great glamour
And is attention captivating.

As I looked through
I caught a glimpse
A glimpse, a glimpse, a glimpse of one in
In ecstasy and dribbling tears.

Yes, contradictory it sounds.
Two extremes in synchrony
Parallel lines meeting
That is typical of the many contradictions
The contradiction that characterises life and nature.

The Sides Of The Truth

Truth has two sides
To hear one and jump to judgement results
Results in misjudgement
Misjudgement and miscarriage of justice.

Every man tells his story
Himself to justify
Except he is above self
Or beyond self
He falls on his sword
The sword of prejudice.

Every story appears true
Until the other side is heard
The evidence weighed
The line is drawn
Good judgement to exercise.

This is the balance
The balance of judgement
For in two opposing sides
The truth may be laying
Laying somewhere midway
And only the hook of sound judgement
One devoid of prejudice, fetch it can.

The Doctor I Know

A constellation of ideals he seems to be
A saver not a saviour
A personage good
The burden bearer
Humane and kind
Gentle but firm.

A good craftsman
Skilful in his art and science
Paying attention to details
Humbled by objectivity
An assessor devoid of prejudice.

He looks as with an eagle's eye
For the signs of disease
Nipping the diagnosis in the bud
He saves his patient the misery of confusion.

A noble man of the noble profession
An erudite scholar
Learning and searching is unending for him
A man of character and dignity
Combining intellectual prowess with prudence
Diligence with assiduity and dexterity
An incurable optimist he is
Given to soundness as a norm.

Inequality

The cry, the cry, the cry
The cry of inequality is as of a roaring lion
Seeking whom to devour.

Is inequality natural or man-made?
Contrived or divine?
Real or imaginary?
Hidden or overt?
The repression is perpetuated
The gap narrow or broad to maintain.

Inequality cries out on the field
On the unlevel playing field made seem level
In the field of unequal equal opportunities
Where the post is shifted according to the winner.
The inclusive law meant to exclude
Like a scale set to serve a hidden agenda
The meter displays a dimorphism.

Man-made inequality is like a primed bomb
Only waiting to explode.
Its deadly ashes spreads
Following after the perpetrators.

The fight against inequality is a fight for all
Basking in its shadows
We all are prone to its evil effects.
The evil menace of the hydra-headed monster
The monster of inequality
Which often comes back to hunt
All in society to hunt.
Inequality, generational or racial
Individualistic or societal
Age related or gender based
Tribal or sectarian
Religious or creed related
Professional or sentimental

Ultimately is like an ill wind
One which blows no good
Serving the expense at the expense of the expense
The gain may be obliterated
And all are at a loss
At a loss to inequality.

The Stillborn

Though resplendent
Lifeless she was born
A life retracted in-utero
Came she noiseless
From the hidden belly of the loved.

There lies a daughter, daughter of zion
The known unknown
The beauty only to be beheld from afar
The expectation aborted
One never to be.

We love her, but can't have her.
We must say goodbye to her
Though the heart aches and tears flow
The loved must be at the requiem
For there, the people will be few.
She was an embodiment of glory
A glory not to be beheld.

Rain

Rain, the falling rain
What blessed freshness it brings
What a blessing from above
A freshness that soothes and strengthens
A freshness unique and divine.

How life depends on you
A blessing indeed you are
The creation of the Lord
The Lord of the universe
How diverse you flow
How wonderful you fall.

The rain gentle and strong
The rain a blessing that can ruin
The rain needed in due season
The rain good in due strength.

In wonder it drops from heaven
Making for drink
And watering the plants
As God sent.

The rain, the rain
The desert cry for thee
The desert desiring to hear
To hear the storms of thunder
The forest is your warm embrace
The forest you beautify in love with comfort.
The rain who can resist
When it pours in measures unmitigated
Mother earth is flooded
The devastation unspeakable
Helpless we watch
Pleading for mercy.
For we can't stop it
Neither can we make it.

The Silent Evening Cloud

The silent evening cloud
A cloud clad in beauty of beauty
Over above it hangs loosely.

Blue and white
Quiet and gentle
It drifts under control
Control of the unseen hand.

In the lofty heights of the sky
It drifts majestically as innocent
What a beauty it portrays as eyes behold
A beauty natural but unfading.

So see I the cloud above
Before it is hidden by nightfall
When perception becomes dull
And the eyelids become droopy.

Good Music

Good music a great delight
A delight that transcends cultural barriers
Music a universal language
It thrills and soothes
Excites and unburdens
Good music a relish for the soul.

Long after the decibel has ceased
It resonates in the heart
Calling and drawing attention to the good melody
The heart is warmed
The spirit ignited
And the body ripples.

The product of ingenious creativity
With which a few are blessed
But to many more it appeals
Good music, ancient as ancient.

Entangled

Entangled, entrapped
Cannot relieve self
Entangled by habit old
Entrapped by wish unabating.

Wishing against wish
Hoping against hope
Fighting against desire hidden
Deliverance far from sight appears.

Man entangled is like a slave
Slaving it out on the alter
The alter of will sacrifice
The sacrifice for appetite unbridled
For appetite unbridled, bridles
Bridles, sowing despair.

Not Alone In The Boat

Not alone in the boat
In the boat of the vicissitudes of life
Of which each has his fair share
But some sure have more than fair a share.

Vicissitudes the product of self action or inaction
Some the result of man's inhumanity to man
Others ensue
Ensue from the nature of nature.

Not alone in the boat
It is rocked softly or harshly
Tossed as unwished
The storm calming comes to pass
At an hour not within easy grasp
Alas consoled, he is not alone
Not alone in the troubled boat of life.

Seeking Answers

In the voyage of life
Questions are constantly raised
Questions to which we seek answers
Questions about the issues of life
Issues perturbing and pervading
Searching questions
To which there are no ready answers.

But man any length will go
Go seeking answers
Willing any price to pay
Thus in searching he may
May find answers
But ironically
He could get lost
Get lost while in search
And the answer elusive remains
While the questions multiply.

Man

Man the good, man the bad
Man the unstable creature
Man the inhuman
Man the double hearted
Man the supreme being.

Man the lover of peace and the provoker of war
Man the free, man the entangled
Man the conqueror, man the slave
Man the encompassed by contradictions
Man the meeting parallels
Man the ambivalent.

Psychological Warfare

Warfare without words
Accomplished in the unseen realm
Unseen but perceptible
Real but can't be substantiated.

A tactical battle
The battle of the matured
Fought with a quiet vehemence
The offensive weapon devoid of offence physical
Potent as potent
In the hand of the skilful
The war without war.

A Child - Joy In The Home

As through the birth canal it comes
Joy fills the home
Joy for a baby born to cuddle.

A child brings joy
Or adds to the joy
The joy and the colour in a home.

Those not blessed by her
Desiring, they bemoan
Seeking the joy theirs to be.

As we watch him grow
We are amazed
The development beholding with enthusiasm
As he joys and jumps around
The noiseless hours he dispels
Leaving us only with the quietude of the sleeping season.

Water

Water a friend to all
The element we can't do without
Important and innocuous it is
When in friendly submission
As daily we find use for it
And our thirst satisfy.

The element everywhere
Falling from above
On the surface it abounds
When we dig deep you are there
With its presence the earth is saturated
But not without a divide.

Saturated but not without divide
Divide into land and body of water
Body of water, the ocean, the sea,
the river, the lake and the spring.
The spring typifying the fountain
The fountain of life water is.

If in scanty supply
We groan for its lack
disease supervenes
And we are at a loss
A substitute unthinkable. When it roars
And a foe becomes
We can't stand its force.
In measures beyond measure
It floods
Untameable it destroys
Leaving us the pieces to pick.

Silenced

The silence of silence
A loud silence
One without ease
The ease of innocence.

When silenced
The inner mouth is closed
The outer is heavy.
A silence of conscience
Leading to the closure of mouth.

Silenced by guilt or by shame
Silenced by belief or by passion
Silenced by objectivity or by sentiment
Silenced by gift or by bribe
Silenced by grief or by greed
Silenced by the bondage of sin
Silenced by fear or by prejudice
Silenced by justice or by injustice
Silenced as though fitted with silencer.

The silence with a disquiet
A flood of disquiet
Pouring through the gateway
Surging through, the silence to break
To break, to achieve
To achieve the silence of the silencer
And the silence of silence
True silence to liberate
Where there is no inner disquiet.

The Animal I Like

The animal I like
The horse the horse
Galloping and galloping
Footsteps audible from distant shores.

Clothed in strength and beauty
Articulate in form and proportions
With senses heeding the masters command.

The horse an animal of worth
One of praise and prestige
Of pride and glamour.

The animal of offence and defence
Taking to the battlefield
A casualty to be or to inflict.
The racing agent
Perfect in strength and stride.
The sporting partner
As the ball we roll.

Devoid of complaint
An animal faithful
Beautiful in character and form
Taking us further where our strength fails
The good partner in progress.

Guilt

Easy to swim into
Difficult the waters to dry off
Pilling it pills
A stronghold to become
Tying down by its strings.

From the simple comes the complex
The guilt complex
And the guilt trap spreading its tentacles
The whole person to enmesh
To enmesh and to hold captive.

Guilt is like a booby trap at times
Set by self
Or by others
We walk into it
Consciously or unaware
The repercussion is the same
Trapped we are entrapped.

Entrapped and struggling free to be
The tentacles may fasten
Ensnaring further down the guilt lane.
Be weary, be cautious
Of the faceless trap
The trap of guilt.

Vain Search

Know, know, know
Find, find, find
Found, found, found
No, no, no
Know not, know not, know not.

In vain search
In vain pursuit
Seem to know
Then know not
The deep longing
Giving not a deep permanent satisfaction
But only a shadowy respite.
The satisfaction longed for
Vaporising after the find
The equilibrium to tilt.

In the end we ask
Ask whether the search is vain vain
Or whether the vain search cease can
Cease, cease.

Vain search a search in vain
Vain search a veiled search
True colour unveiled after the find.
Vain search a search as searching for a mirage
After the find, it disappears
And the void void persists.
Vain search a reflection
Reflecting the futility of life
And the evasiveness of permanent fulfilment.

Malice

Malice the grave
The grave of the psychologically immature
And the spiritually bankrupt
Ill informed
And ill equipped
The overcome go down the depraved lane of malice.

Going down the lane ill willed
Moving in rancour and inner turbulence.
Sighting the opponent
The bitterness wells up
Wells up like surging molten lava
Sooner or later the volcano erupts
Spewing forth its rock.

Those playing its game
Are neither children nor mature
As if caught in the middle of nowhere
Paddling in unpleasant waters
In waters devoid of a refreshing power.

From the boundaries of such waters
The distance is better kept
Better kept, better avoided.
For its water, the waters of despair become
Failing the wound to heal
Only deepening the sore of acrimony.

Living In the Past

Some are so detached and attached
They are living in the past
Living in the past
The past of life
As if entangled, can't move on
Bound to the past as though to the present.

Wallowing in the joys
In the joys and errors of the past
Lost in the pool of memories
Which does no good to the present.
Failing to move on, they move backwards.
Move backwards as the world moves on
For the ticking clock of progress waits for no one.

Catch up, obsolete not to be.
For the evil and good of yesterday are gone
The regrets and missed opportunities of yesteryears
have slipped away
Consigned as to a coffin
They are sealed for good.

Living in the past
Attached to the evil of yesterday
Detached from the good of today and morrow
Life becomes a drag and a struggle
The savour lost, lost to the past.

Obsession

The varying idiosyncrasy
Compelling like a force
The bizarre to do.
The plunge taken in repetition
Helpless, the subject can't resist
Falling with eyes wide opened.

Propelled as though blown by the wind
Like a leaf to unsavoury destinations
Having no say
Unable to exact will/wish.

At the mercy of the object
The object of obsession
Like a man in captivity
Devoid of self assertion.
Blown like a leaf
By the wind of obsession
Dangling to the dictates of the object.

The objects of obsession vary
Varying from the simple to the complex
From the common to the uncommon
From the subnormal to the abnormal
From the obvious to the bizarre.

The bondage of self to self by self
Yielding the cycle of entanglements
Like a fish trapped in a net
Needing help free to be
Welcome the help; free, free
Free to become.

Tinted

Tinted, tinted, tinted
Man imperfect is tinted
The tinge not obvious
In all resides.

However good
However bad
Not absolutely good
Not absolutely bad
The tint in all reside.
The bad in the midst of good
The good in the midst of bad
The blending or unblending contrast.

The contrast of light and darkness
For where there is light there is shadow
And where there is shadow there is darkness
Likened to the darkness of light
And to the lightness of the dark.
Thus absolute lightness or absolute darkness
A breach of reality only remains.

Man, man, tinted man
Man is tinted
The tint positive or negative
In man not infallible reside.

Victims Of Crime

The pain inflicted
The blood spilled
The emotions shattered
The form maimed beyond repair
Prices paid to crime by victims, incalculable.

Victims of crime
Innocent victims
Or victims of innocence
Victims of their own misgivings
Or victims of victims
In the rolling wheel of crime.

The victims of crime
The victims of triple jeopardy
After the public glare
Left to self the pieces to pick.
After being victims of crime
The victims of injustice may turn
Becoming the victims of the injustice of justice.
Helpless they groan in despair
Knowing not where else to turn.

Injustice

Rampant, rampant
Rampant as the blue sky
Flying over or crawling
Overt or cryptic
Injustice unsettles
Unsettles the harbour where it docks.

A connotation of weakness
The weakness of the strong
Who in strength and disguise
Tramples over the victim.

Injustice is often coloured
Coloured in blue as a reflection of weakness
The advantage of the weak taken.
The weak and the helpless
Overrun and outwitted
Lying in the despair of despair.

Coloured in red as an excuse
The injustice of justice and the justice of injustice
An excuse for a fierce restraint.
The anger blossoms
The hatred to fuel
For at the root of injustice is hatred red hot
Or the dying embers of prejudice fanned to flame.
Where there is injustice either is present
Present, present as a must
Justice to twist.

Emotion

Emotion, the human emotion
Rich and diverse
Profound and varied
Transcending planes palpable.

Varying from man to man
From man to woman
From childhood to adulthood
From phase to phase in the journey
The journey of life.

How varied is the human emotion?
In the broad divergent
In the fine, finite.
As unique as fingerprints
Varying as the self nonsense DNA sequence
Tending towards the senselessness of emotion
Unpredictable and uncurtailable at times.

The swing, the stability
The stability, the swing
The mix of emotions unfettered
Non singular but plural
Overlapping in the spectrum band.
The fire stoked bellows
Bellows the light to glow.

The human emotion
Is a weapon of grace
Which to mischief can turn
Turning the turn
A twist to untie.

The Voice of Prejudice

A distant voice moaning
Moaning audibly
The prejudice to echo aloud
Aloud, aloud, echo aloud.

A voice blind to reasoning or soundness
In the darkness of blindness
Can't see
Unwilling to see
Doubly blind.

The ears as closed as deaf
Can't hear the argument.
The mind sealed as deluded
Can't shift ground
The facts to weigh.

Bent on presumption
The assumption is reinforced
Rigid as bronze casted
Formed, formed
When strong, strong
The mould is no longer malleable/pliable
Then flourish only can.
The illusion insensitive to facts
Insensitive even to hard cold facts
The unforged data notwithstanding
The resonance is unabated.

The Colourless Man

The inner man
The colourless man
Hidden within the coloured outer case
Unconfined to shape, colour or form.

The colourless man
Invisible at arms length
The spirit within distant distant
Good or bad
The colourless man is the true self
the true self, the true you/me.

The colourless man
The character, the gem
The quality, the disdain
The good, the evil
The stony, the muddy
Which relevance bears no
To the coloured outer man.

Its beauty, the attraction
Its evil, the repugnance
Whose shade from distance can't see.
Colourless and invisible
Hidden from the outside world
In the crevice of the outer man.
The inner man shielded
Is the colourless man
The colourless and the real man.

In A Moment Of Madness

Every man fallible is at risk
At risk, at risk, at risk of the spill
The spill like milk boiling over
Of uttercation unguarded
And of conduct undignified.

In a moment of madness
Seized and off guard
The verbal aggression poured out
The unfitting conduct displayed.

Like raw eggs broken
So are the unprintable spoken
Can't be retrieved
Can't be revamped
The break broken can't be mended.

Like fish out of water
So is the atypical conduct displayed in a fit
Thereafter the action like dust dispersed
Can't be reassembled.

Beware, beweary
Beware of the moment
The moment a moment of madness
For when seized by its whims
By its whims and caprices
The mortals fall
Fall, fall, they fall.
In the moment of madness they fall
Fall below low.

The Poet

The literary composer
Given to diction, imagery and rhythm
A genius of clarity or unclarity
Rich in expression
Searching the deep
The real and the abstract to poetize.

He writes to echo
To echo deep distant thoughts
From depths of imagination beyond imagination
With an intensity searching.

The poet, the thinker
Given to conventional and unconventional wisdom.
Thinking afloat
Like a wood adrift on sea.
As though alien
Seeing at times from a perspective dotty.

He writes to point
To point as if appointed
Appointed to be the conscience of society.
Evoking the subconscious
That the petals of truth and good might fan out
Fan out, their beauty to spread.

Man and Woman

Man, free to be masculine
Woman, free to be feminine
In the freedom of acceptance
The acceptance of self and the other
We find liberty.

Man a symbol of character and strength
Subsumed in his own world
In and out he strays
As though attached and detached.

Woman an epitome of beauty and passion
Clothed in strength and weakness
The strength of weakness
The weakness as strength.

Women our mothers
The mother of fathers
And of heroes
Who in the strength of weakness
Birthed and nursed the men strong
Therefore self strong, strong.

Man and woman in contention
A needless contention
Complementary partners are
Not rivals in the field of life
Each having pride of place
Each strong in his or her own right.

The strife, the variance
The discontent, the emulation
Only lead down the path
The path of ultimate decline.

Printed in the United Kingdom
by Lightning Source UK Ltd.
103032UKS00001B/85-99